THE PRESIDENTS

by Campbell Collison

Minneapolis, Minnesota

Credits:
© Cover: clockwise from bottom left, Everett-Art/Shutterstock; Independent birds/Shutterstock; prapass/Shutterstock; Everett Historical/Shutterstock; Alexander Sviridov/Shutterstock; Sashluk/Shutterstock; The Library of Congress/Public Domain; 4, Howard Chandler Christy/Public Domain; 5 top, Jean Leon Gerome Ferris/Public Domain; 5 bottom middle, M. Unal Ozmen/Shutterstock; 5 left, The Library of Congress/Public Domain; 5 bottom right, Gilbert Stuart/Public Domain; 6 bottom, Courtesy of the George W. Bush Presidential Library/Public Domain; 6 top left, Gilbert Stuart/Public Domain; 6 top right, George Peter Alexander Healy/Public Domain; 7 top center, Public Domain; 7 top, clockwise: Constant Mayer/Public Domain; John Vanderlyn/Public Domain; Gilbert Stuart/Public Domain; John Singer Sargent/Public Domain; Gilbert Stuart/Public Domain; George Peter Alexander Healy/Public Domain; 7 bottom left, U.S. National Archives and Records Administration/Public Domain; 8 left, Harris & Ewing/Public Domain; 8 bottom left, cynoclub/Shutterstock; 8 middle, Eliphalet Frazer Andrews/Public Domain; 8 bottom right, Gilbert Stuart/Public Domain; 8 right, Boonchuay Promjiam/Shutterstock; 9 top, Library of Congress/Public Domain; 9 left, Elmer Wesley Greene/Public Domain; 9 middle, Richard Marsden Brown/Public Domain; 9 right, Official White House Photo by Chuck Kennedy/Public Domain; 10, United States Mint/Public Domain; 10, George Peter Alexander Healy/Public Domain; 10, Rembrandt Peale/Public Domain; 11 right, John Trumbull; 11 top left, Frank Graham Cootes/Public Domain; 11 left middle, National Archives and Records Administration; 11 left bottom, George Peter Alexander Healy; 11 top right, Ralph Eleaser Whiteside Earl/Public Domain; 11 bottom middle, Gift of Beatrice Perskie Foxman and Dr. Stanley B. Foxman/Creative Commons;12 bottom, Executive Office of the President of the United States/Public Domain; 12 top, NASA/Public Domain; 13 middle, John Chester Buttre/Public Domain; 13 bottom left, John Singer Sargent/Public Domain; 13 top left, Michal Chmurski/Shutterstock; 13 right, D. Edwin/Public Domain; 14, Executive Office of the President/Public Domain; 15 top, Official White House Photo by Pete Souza/Public Domain; 15 bottom left, Library of Congress/Public Domain; 15 bottom right, White House Photographic Office/Public Domain; 16 left, Edward Savage/Public Domain; 16 middle, Prostock-studio/Shutterstock.com; 16 right middle, George Peter Alexander Healy/Public Domain; 17 left, George H.W. Bush Presidential Library and Museum, Courtesy of US Army Golden Knights Parachute Team/Public Domain; 17 right, Library of Congress/Public Domain; 18 left, Sippman/Shutterstock; 18 bottom left, Alexander Gardner/Public Domain; 18 bottom right, NASA/Public Domain; 19 top, George H.W. Bush Presidential Library and Museum/NARA/Public Domain; 19 left, The White House/Public Domain; 19 left, s_bukley/Shutterstock.com; 19 bottom, photomaster/Shutterstock; 20, Doris A. and Lawrence H. Budner Theodore Roosevelt Collection, DeGolyer Library, Southern Methodist University/Public Domain; 20 bottom, kite studio/Shutterstock; 21 top, Kamira/Shutterstock.com; 21 bottom left, Roberto La Rosa/Shutterstock; 21 bottom middle, Library of Congress/Public Domain; 21 bottom right, Roberto La Rosa/Shutterstock; 22 Gerald R. Ford Presidential Library/Public Domain; 23 top, White House (Pete Souza)/Public Domain; 23 bottom left, Doris A. and Lawrence H. Budner Collection/Public Domain; 23 bottom middle, WeAre/Shutterstock; 23 bottom right Library of Congress/Public Domain; 24 bottom Cecil W. Stoughton/U.S. National Archives and Records Administration/Public Domain; 24 left, Bob McNeely/White House Photograph Office; 25 top background Angelo Cordeschi/Shutterstock.com; 25 top left, Jean Leon Gerome Ferris/Public Domain; 25 top right George Peter Alexander Healy/Public Domain; 25 bottom left andrewvect/Shutterstock; 25 bottom middle, Tatiana Popova/Shutterstock; 25 bottom right, U.S. military/Public Domain; 26, Alexander Gardner/Civil War Glass Negatives/Public Domain; 26 right, Library of Congress/Public Domain; 27 top, Pete Souza/Public Domain; 27 bottom left, NASA/Public Domain; 27 bottom right, NASA Robert Markowitz, Mark Sowa/Public Domain; 27 midlle left, Public Domain/Andrii Spy_k/Shutterstock; 27 midlle right, Retouch man/Shutterstock; 28 left, Everett Historical/Shutterstock; 29 right, Roman Samborskyi/Shutterstock; 28-29, Austen Photography

Developed and produced for Bearport Publishing by BlueAppleWorks Inc.
Managing Editor for BlueAppleWorks: Melissa McClellan
Art Director: T.J. Choleva
Photo Research: Jane Reid
Editor: Marcia Abramson

Library of Congress Cataloging-in-Publication Data

Names: Collison, Campbell, author.
Title: The Presidents / by Campbell Collison.
Other titles: United States presidents
Description: Minneapolis, Minnesota : Bearport Publishing Company, [2021] | Series: Xtreme facts: U.S. history | Includes bibliographical references and index.
Identifiers: LCCN 2020012911 (print) | LCCN 2020012912 (ebook) | ISBN 9781647471217 (library binding) | ISBN 9781647471286 (paperback) | ISBN 9781647471354 (ebook)
Subjects: LCSH: Presidents—United States—Miscellanea—Juvenile literature.
Classification: LCC E176.8 .C65 2021 (print) | LCC E176.8 (ebook) | DDC 973.09/9—dc23
LC record available at https://lccn.loc.gov/2020012911
LC ebook record available at https://lccn.loc.gov/2020012912

For more information, write to Bearport Publishing, 5357 Penn Avenue South, Minneapolis, MN 55419.
Printed in the United States of America.

Contents

Help Wanted: A President!

When the United States became a new nation, it didn't have a president! The new country's government had been created with a weak **federal** government that had no central leader. But the people soon realized they needed someone in charge.

So, they wrote the U.S. **Constitution**, which created the role of president to lead the nation. In 1789, George Washington was elected by **unanimous** vote.

George Washington didn't want to be president. He wanted to retire!

In 1787, Washington led the Constitutional Convention as it decided on the rights of the nation's citizens and established how the U.S. government would work.

President Washington was elected for a second term as president in 1792.

Washington was sworn into his second term in Philadelphia, which was the U.S. capital from 1790 to 1800.

Washington loved ice cream. There were no cones when he was alive. Instead, ice cream was served in small cups known as ice pots.

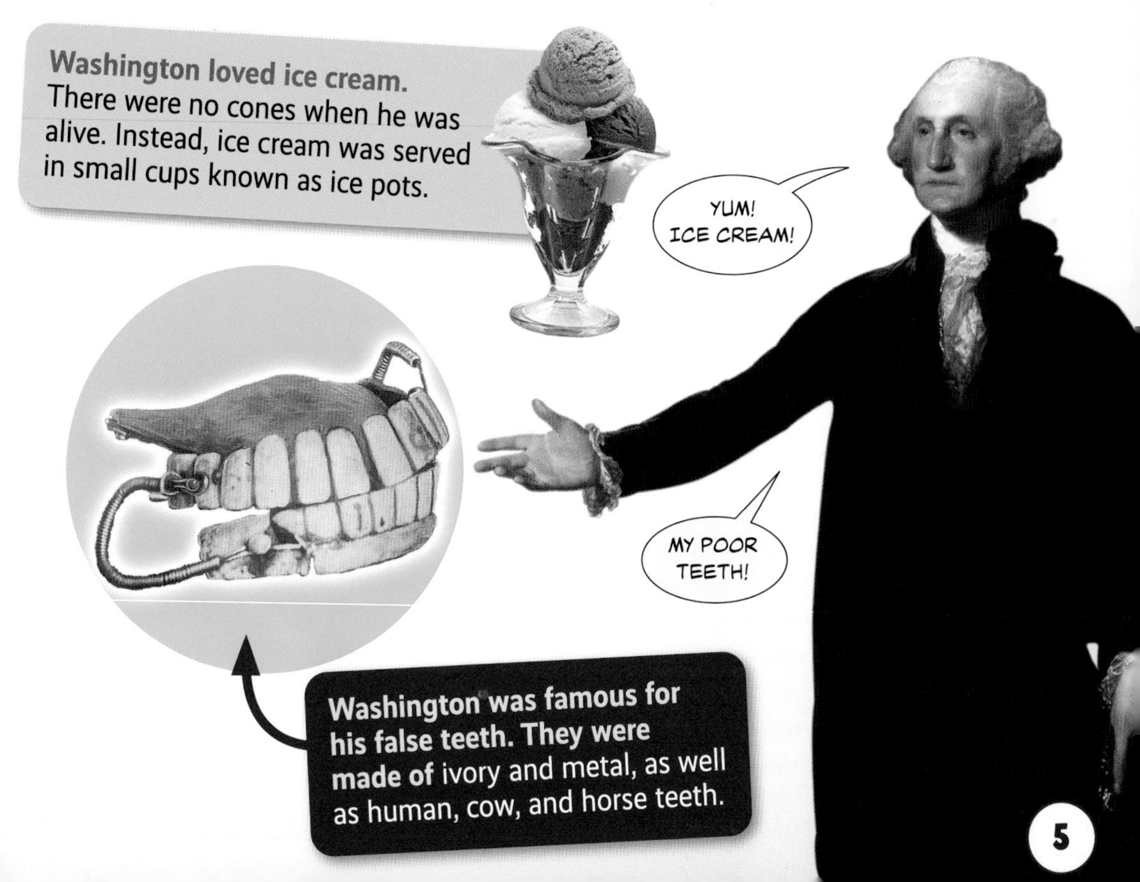
YUM! ICE CREAM!
MY POOR TEETH!

Washington was famous for his false teeth. They were made of ivory and metal, as well as human, cow, and horse teeth.

All in the (President's) Family

Sometimes the United States presidency is like a family business. Several cousins and two father-and-son pairs have served as president. Benjamin Harrison took office 48 years after his grandfather, William Henry Harrison, was president. Presidents Theodore Roosevelt and Franklin Delano Roosevelt were distant cousins and were related to many past presidents!

John Adams
John Quincy Adams
THIS IS MY OFFICE NOW, 41!
UP TOP, 43!

John Adams was the second president, and **his oldest son**, John Quincy Adams, **became the sixth president.**

President **George H. W. Bush**, the 41st president, and his son President **George W. Bush**, the 43rd president, are often referred to simply as 41 and 43.

George H. W. Bush often dropped by the White House for a chat when George W. Bush was president.

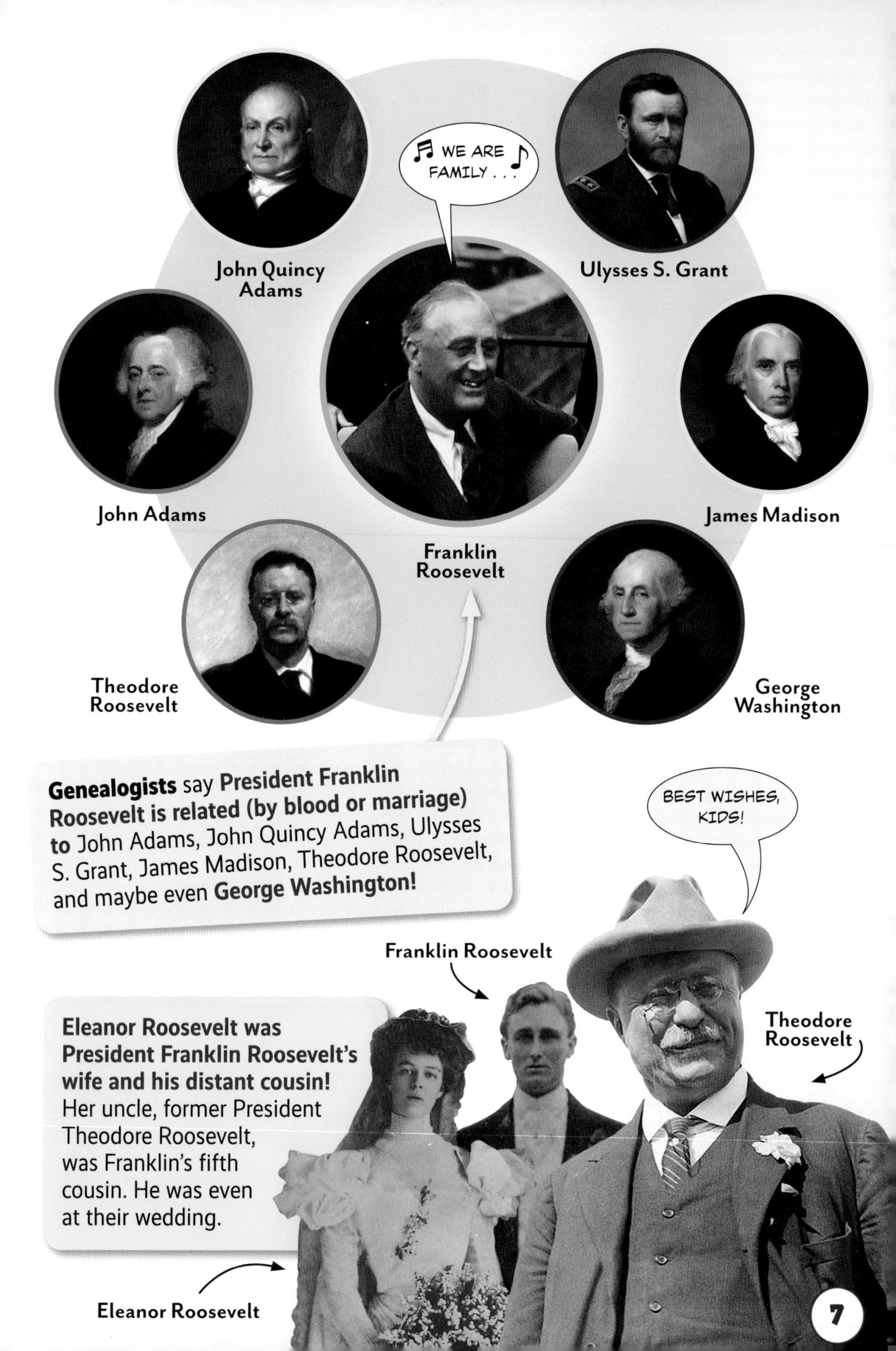

Genealogists say **President Franklin Roosevelt is related (by blood or marriage) to** John Adams, John Quincy Adams, Ulysses S. Grant, James Madison, Theodore Roosevelt, and maybe even **George Washington!**

Eleanor Roosevelt was President Franklin Roosevelt's wife and his distant cousin! Her uncle, former President Theodore Roosevelt, was Franklin's fifth cousin. He was even at their wedding.

Ladies First, Gentlemen!

As wife of the president, Martha Washington's duties included hosting social gatherings. She was sometimes referred to as our Lady Presidentess. The role of the First Lady has changed over time. Today, in addition to party-planning duties, First Ladies focus on important social issues and causes. But one thing hasn't changed—First Ladies don't get paid!

President Woodrow Wilson's second wife, Edith, took on much of the president's work while he recovered from a stroke that left him partly **paralyzed** and nearly blind in one eye.

The term First Lady was first used in 1849 when President Zachary Taylor honored Dolley Madison, wife of President James Madison, at her funeral.

First Ladies **Martha Washington and Dolley Madison both had pet parrots.**

I AM THE WASHINGTONS' COCKATOO!

Only one First Lady had her wedding at the White House. Frances Folsom and Grover Cleveland married there in 1886.

Ruth, the Clevelands' first child, was born in 1891. The public loved baby Ruth so much they named a candy bar after her!

President Herbert Hoover and First Lady Lou Henry often spoke to each other in **Chinese** so other people wouldn't know what they were saying!
Michelle Obama was the first African American First Lady of the United States.
我爱你
ME, TOO.
HE SAID, "I LOVE YOU." HOW SWEET!

The Faces of Money

It wasn't until the Civil War (1861–1865) that the United States government began issuing paper money. Alexander Hamilton got his face on the $10 bill because he was the first Secretary of the Treasury. Founding Father and inventor Benjamin Franklin is the only other non-president on U.S. paper money—the $100 bill. Today's money is covered with many familiar presidential faces.

Abraham Lincoln is on our $5 bill and was the first president to appear on a coin. It was called the **Lincoln penny**.

George Washington is one of only three presidents on both a coin and a bill.

Thomas Jefferson is on the nickel and the rarely used $2 bill.

The largest bill ever made featured President Woodrow Wilson.

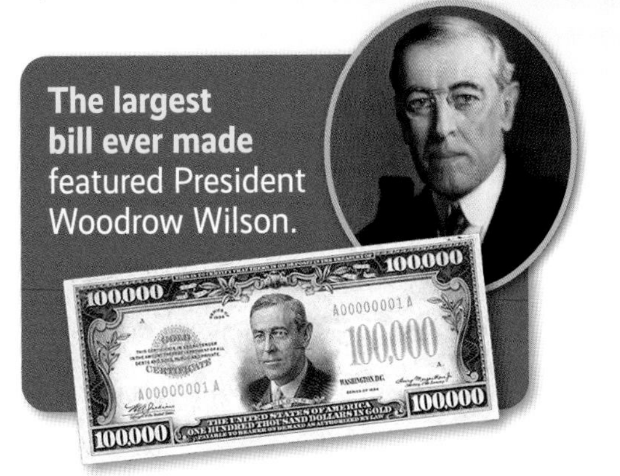

Andrew Jackson, the seventh president, has been on the $20 bill since 1928.

President John F. Kennedy was honored on the half-dollar after he was **assassinated** in 1963.

Washington did not want his image to appear on money. He felt that was something that kings did, and he **didn't want to be treated like a king.**

The $50 bill features the 18th **president, Ulysses S. Grant.** A $50 bill wears out in about 8.5 years!

The Franklin Roosevelt dime came out on January 30, 1946, his first birthday after he died in office.

An image of Harriet Tubman, the **abolitionist**, has been proposed for a new $20 bill. She **would be the first woman on a U.S. bill.**

Measuring Up

You might say serving as president is a tall order. The last six men to hold office have all been taller than the average height for U.S. men. Presidents Ronald Reagan, Bill Clinton, and Barack Obama were all 6 feet 1 inch (185 cm) tall. President George H. W. Bush was 6 ft 2 in (188 cm) tall, while his son, President George W. Bush, measured 6 ft (183 cm). President Donald Trump is 6 ft 3 in (190.5 cm) tall. How else do the U.S. presidents measure up?

John F. Kennedy was the youngest elected president at age 43.

The oldest elected president so far is Donald Trump. He was 70 years old at his **inauguration** ceremony.

Donald Trump stood tall as he took the oath of office on January 20, 2017. He is the third-tallest U.S. president.

Abraham Lincoln was **the tallest president**, measuring 6 ft 4 in (193 cm) tall.

I HAVE THE BIGGEST PRESIDENTIAL FEET EVER. I WEAR SIZE 14 SHOES!

James Madison was **the shortest president**, measuring 5 ft 4 in (162.5 cm).

SO? I WEAR A SIZE 7.25 HAT!

Theodore Roosevelt was only 42 when he took office after President William McKinley was killed.

I MAY BE YOUNG, BUT I AM READY!

Left-Handed and Proud of It

While only about 10 percent of people in the United States hold a pen or toss a ball with their left hand, 8 of the 45 U.S. presidents have been lefties. That's almost 18 percent! In fact, 5 of the last 8 presidents were left-handed, including Gerald Ford, George H. W. Bush, Bill Clinton, and Barack Obama. President Ronald Reagan is also on the left-handed list. He was a natural lefty but learned to write with his right hand as a child.

In the past, teachers often forced children who were left-handed to write with their right hand.

President Harry S. Truman did many things with his left hand, including throwing out the first pitch at this baseball game.

Truman threw out the first pitch before a Washington Senators game in 1952.

When **Barack Obama** signed his first three documents as president, he joked, **"I'm a lefty. Get used to it!"**

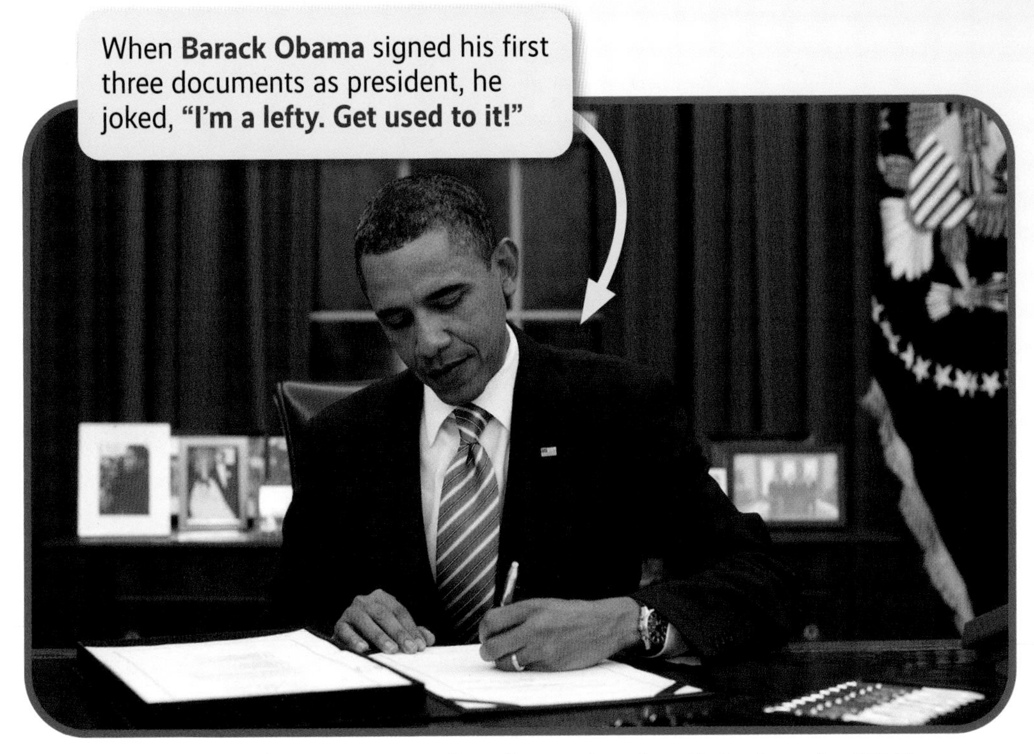

Obama used many pens to sign a food safety law in 2011. Presidents often give out signing pens as souvenirs.

James Garfield is said to be the **first left-handed president**, but he could write with both hands.

President Ronald Reagan was also left-handed. But, just like President Garfield, he learned to switch at an early age.

I CAN WRITE WITH BOTH HANDS!
JOIN THE CLUB!

Happy Birthday, Mr. President!

February may be the shortest month, but it includes some important presidential birthdays. It's also when the nation celebrates Presidents' Day. George Washington's birthday on February 22 was chosen for the school holiday celebration in 1879. But some wanted the holiday to honor both George Washington and Abraham Lincoln, who was born on February 12. Presidents' Day is now celebrated on the third Monday of the month, falling right between the two birthdays.

ENJOY THE DAY OFF, KIDS!
THANKS FROM ALL THE KIDS IN AMERICA!
HOW THOUGHTFUL.
James Monroe
Calvin Coolidge

George Washington

Abraham Lincoln

Presidents **Calvin Coolidge** and **James Monroe** share birthdays with the nation! They were born on the 4th of July.

President **Franklin Roosevelt** once celebrated his birthday with a **toga** party at the White House.

The Roosevelts dressed like Romans after critics said the president acted like an emperor.

George H. W. Bush celebrated his 90th birthday by parachuting out of an airplane!

In 1920, **Warren G. Harding** was elected president on his birthday—November 2.

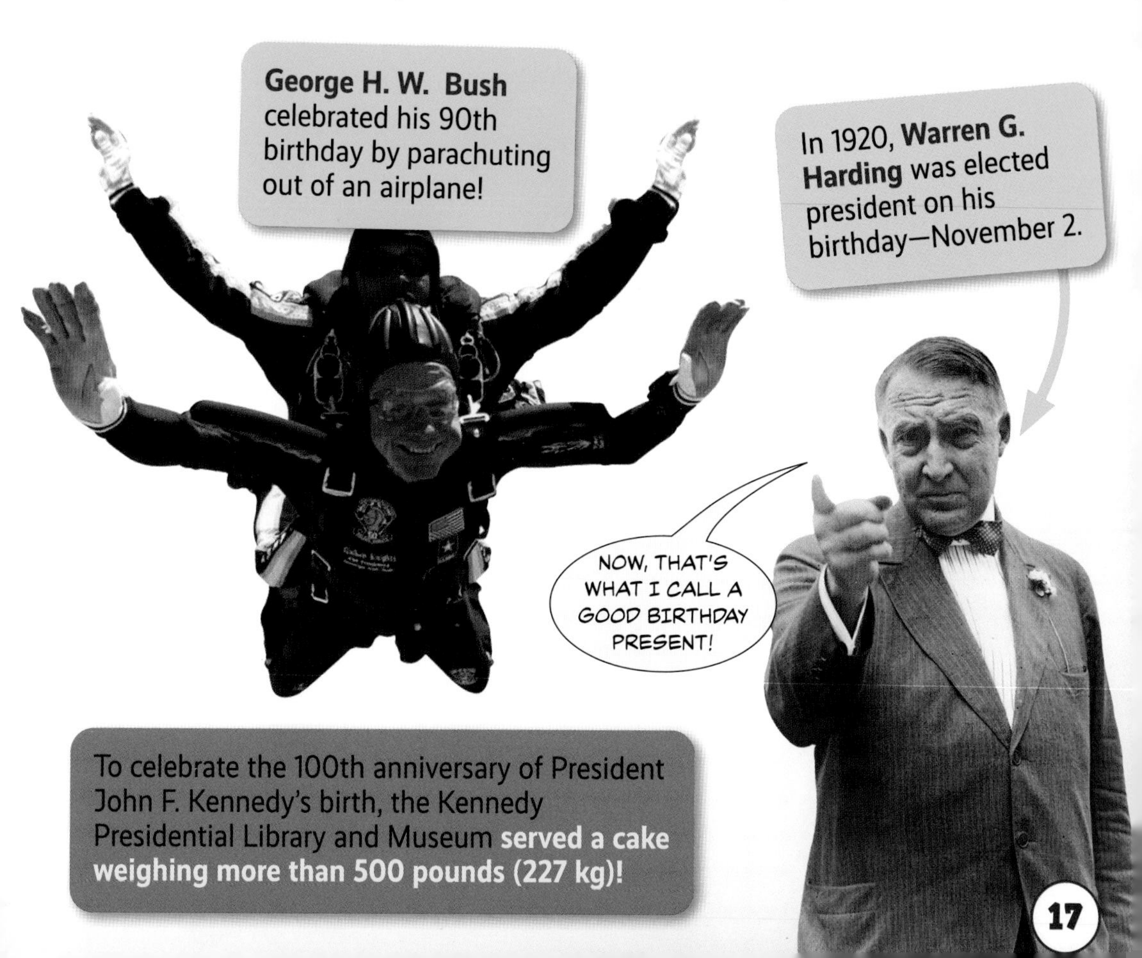

NOW, THAT'S WHAT I CALL A GOOD BIRTHDAY PRESENT!

To celebrate the 100th anniversary of President John F. Kennedy's birth, the Kennedy Presidential Library and Museum **served a cake weighing more than 500 pounds (227 kg)!**

Turkey Pardons

It has become traditional for presidents to **pardon** turkeys in the days before Thanksgiving. It may have started with President Abraham Lincoln. His son Tad had grown attached to a turkey that had been given to the family for their Christmas meal. Tad named the bird Jack and begged his father to spare the turkey's life. Lincoln agreed, and Jack became Tad's pet.

The turkey pardoning tradition got a **big boost from First Lady Patricia Nixon** who sent a pardoned turkey to live on a farm.

GOOD IDEA!
I WANT TO KEEP JACK AS MY PET, DAD.
ABSOLUTELY, TAD!

When **President John F. Kennedy** was presented with a turkey, he **decided to return the bird rather than eat it**. The **media** first used the term pardon while reporting on the event.

President George H. W. Bush once declared, "This fine tom turkey . . . will not end up on anyone's dinner table. . . . He's granted a presidential pardon!"

President Barack Obama referred to each year's pardoned turkey as the **TOTUS, or Turkey of the United States.**

HOW IS THE TOTUS DOING?
ALL IS GREAT HERE. THANK YOU, **POTUS**!

In 2009, President **Obama sent two pardoned turkeys to Disneyland** to live out their days.

The White House Zoo

Most presidents and their families have had pets while living in the White House. President Barack Obama got his daughters a puppy to thank them for their support during his run for president. George H. W. Bush's spaniel Millie wrote a best-selling book about being a first pet (with help from First Lady Barbara Bush). Theodore Roosevelt's kids had guinea pigs, lizards, badgers, snakes, pigs, a hyena, a pony, a one-legged rooster, and a small bear!

Theodore Roosevelt's sons, **Quentin and Kermit, once brought their family's pony on the White House elevator** to visit their brother Archie, who was sick with the measles.

Quentin Roosevelt once interrupted a White House meeting to show his father some snakes he had bought.

Theodore Roosevelt had four sons and two daughters.

THEY (WHO) SEEK TO ESTABLISH
SYSTEMS OF GOVERNMENT BASED ON
THE REGIMENTATION OF ALL HUMAN
BEINGS BY A HANDFUL OF INDIVIDUAL
RULERS... CALL THIS A NEW ORDER.
IT IS NOT NEW AND IT IS NOT ORDER.

Franklin Roosevelt's beloved **Scottish terrier, Fala**, sits by his side at the president's memorial in Washington, D.C.

Fala became so famous that he had his own secretary to answer fan mail!

President **Andrew Johnson fed the white mice** he found in his White House bedroom!

President **Abraham Lincoln declined the** King of Siam's **offer of a gift of elephants.**

President Herbert Hoover's son Allan had alligators in their family home before his father was elected president.

Good Sports

It's not unusual for winners of elections to also be winners in sports. Many of our nation's presidents have worked hard and played hard. From the expert **equestrian** George Washington and basketball enthusiast Barack Obama, to college football star Gerald Ford and dedicated golfer Donald Trump, presidents often shine in their favorite sports.

President **George W. Bush was a cheerleader** at his high school and at Yale University.

President Richard Nixon had a one-lane bowling alley built in the White House.

Gerald Ford was named Most Valuable Player for his college football team.

When **President Barack Obama** took office in 2009, he had the White House tennis court converted into a basketball court.

President Obama liked to practice his shots on the White House lawn. His daughters Malia and Sasha often joined in.

Abraham Lincoln was the wrestling champion of his Illinois county. He was only defeated once.
WHO IS TOUGHER, KID?

I COULD TAKE YOU, TEDDY!

After a Hard Day at the Office

Presidents don't have much spare time for hobbies while they are serving the country. But many have found ways to unwind after a busy and stressful day in the **Oval Office**. George Washington enjoyed dancing, and Theodore Roosevelt liked to walk on stilts. Several presidents were musical. Harry S. Truman loved to play the piano, and Bill Clinton was skilled on the saxophone.

LET'S PLAY OUR FAVORITE SONG.
YES, "HAIL TO THE CHIEF"!

In 2017, former **President George W. Bush published a best-selling book** of his own paintings.

I CAN SPEAK FRENCH, LATIN, ITALIAN, GREEK, SPANISH, AND GERMAN.

HMM, I ONLY SPEAK FRENCH, DUTCH, GERMAN, AND LATIN.

Thomas Jefferson spoke **six languages!**

John Quincy Adams swam **in the Potomac River every morning—without a swimsuit!**

President Harry S. Truman had poker chips with the presidential seal printed on them.

I WIN AGAIN!

While serving in World War II (1939–1945), **Richard Nixon** is said to have **won enough money** at card games **to help pay for his first run for Congress.**

From Telegraph To Twitter

Technology has transformed the presidency. President Franklin Roosevelt used the radio to reassure a worried nation that was battered by the **Great Depression** and World War II. Television made its mark in 1960 when the broadcast debate between a young and handsome John F. Kennedy and a nervous and sweaty Richard Nixon may have helped swing the vote in Kennedy's favor. Today, we get presidential news within seconds, delivered by Facebook and Twitter.

President Abraham Lincoln relied on the **telegraph** to get speedy reports from Civil War battlefields.

President Rutherford B. Hayes made the first presidential telephone call in the White House.

Barack Obama became the first president to go live on Twitter.

With news reporters watching, President Obama sent out the first presidential tweets.

Franklin Roosevelt was the first president to appear on television.

When the White House installed electric lights in 1891, **President Benjamin Harrison was afraid of being electrocuted.** He wouldn't touch the light switches.

In 1999, President **Bill Clinton** and Astronaut **John Glenn** exchanged emails between Earth and outer space!

SO, WHAT'S UP IN SPACE?

WELL . . . I AM!

Look Like Lincoln

CRAFT PROJECT

President Lincoln is known for his stovepipe hat and beard. Yet he didn't grow the beard until 1860! A girl of 11, Grace Bedell, from Westfield, New York, wrote to the future president and suggested he grow a beard. She thought it would help him win the election. He took her advice! Make your own beard and hat mask to look positively presidential.

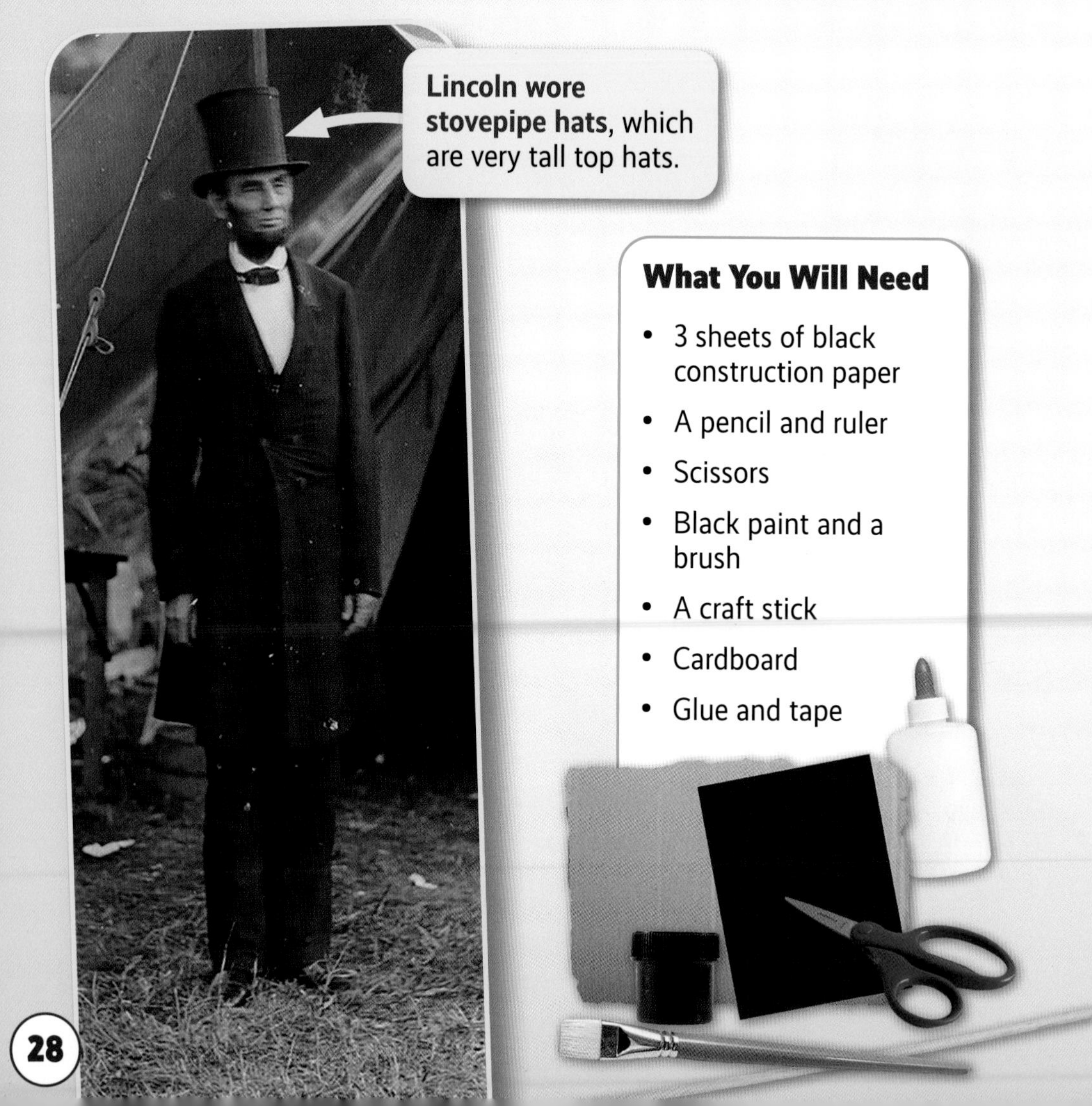

Lincoln wore stovepipe hats, which are very tall top hats.

What You Will Need

- 3 sheets of black construction paper
- A pencil and ruler
- Scissors
- Black paint and a brush
- A craft stick
- Cardboard
- Glue and tape

Step One

On a sheet of black construction paper, draw an oval about the size of your face. Draw a smaller oval inside the first one, making a curved line about about ¼ in (0.6 cm) thick. At one end of the oval, draw a long, thin rectangle. It should be longer than the oval. Cut the pieces out.

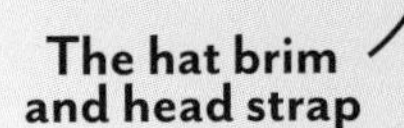

Step Two

Take another sheet of black paper and draw a larger rectangle that is about the same width and height as your oval. Cut out the rectangle.

The hat's stovepipe top

Step Three

Cut long strips of construction paper about 1 in (2.6 cm) wide. Cut the strip into small pieces of paper, about ¼ inch (0.6 cm) long. These will be your whiskers.

Whiskers

Step Four

A craft stick

Paint the craft stick with black paint. Leave to dry.

Step Five

Glue the paper from steps 1 and 2 onto a piece of cardboard. Let the glue dry and cut the shapes out. Glue the tall stovepipe section to the top of the hat brim section. Glue the whisker strips to the bottom of the head strap to create the beard. Tape the end of the craft stick to the back of the hat brim. Hold the stick in your hand and position the mask in front of your face for great pictures!

Glossary

abolitionist a person who wants to stop or abolish slavery

assassinated killed in a surprise attack

constitution a basic statement of laws and principles

convention a meeting of people to work toward a common goal

critics people who find fault

equestrian a horseback rider

federal having to do with the national government; not the state or local government

genealogists people who study family ancestry and history

Great Depression a period in the 1930s when many people in the United States lost their jobs and were very poor

inauguration the ceremony and celebration to install someone in office or begin something new

media the system and organizations of communication through which information is spread to a large number of people

Oval Office the room, named for its shape, where the president works

paralyzed unable to move

pardon to forgive someone for a crime, which prevents any punishment, including the death penalty

POTUS the President of the United States

spar to practice boxing

telegraph an electronic machine that sent coded messages

toga a loosely wrapped garment that was worn in ancient Rome

unanimous when all people in a group agree about one particular matter or vote the same way

Connors, Kathleen. *What Does the President Do? (A Look at Your Government).* New York: Gareth Stevens (2018).

Mihaly, Christy. *Ask the President (Governing the United States).* North Mankato, MN: Rourke Educational Media (2020).

Palmer, Erin. *U.S. Presidents (Really Weird, Totally True Facts About . . .).* Vero Beach, FL: Rourke Educational Media (2017).

1. Go to **www.factsurfer.com**
2. Enter "**Presidents**" into the search box.
3. Click on the cover of this book to see a list of websites.

Index

About the Author

Campbell Collison is the pseudonym for Cathy Collison and Janis Campbell. The two Michigan writers are both married and have two grown children each. They are avid history tourists and love uncovering fun facts, whether traveling to historic homes, presidential libraries, or national parks across the country. The friends have been writing partners for 25 years.